W9-BTB-002

Playing a Game

Inclined Plane vs. Lever

by Mari Schuh

first step nonfiction

Lerner Publications · Minneapolis

LERNER

SOURCE

Expand learning beyond the printed book. Download free, complementary educational resources for this book from our website, www.lerneresource.com.

All images in this book are used with the permission of: © Todd Strand/Independent Picture Service except: © iStockphoto.com/manley099, p. 7; © Shariff Che\' Lah/Dreamstime.com, p. 8 (bottom left); © iStockphoto.com/simonkr, p. 8 (top right); © iStockphoto.com/venturecx, p. 8 (top left); iStockphoto.com/Eerik, p. 13; © iStockphoto.com/Krakozawr, p. 14.

Front cover: © Todd Strand/Independent Picture Service.

Main body text set in ITC Avant Garde Gothic Std Medium 21/25.
Typeface provided by Adobe Systems.

Lerner Publications Company
A division of Lerner Publishing Group, Inc.
241 First Avenue North
Minneapolis, MN 55401 USA

For reading levels and more information, look up this title at www.lernerbooks.com.

Library of Congress Cataloging-in-Publication Data

Schuh, Mari C., 1975– author.
    Playing a game : inclined plane vs. lever / by Mari Schuh.
        pages cm — (First step nonfiction. Simple machines to the rescue)
    Audience: Ages 5-8
    Audience: K to grade 3
    ISBN 978-1-4677-8027-8 (lb : alk. paper) — ISBN 978-1-4677-8296-8 (pb : alk. paper) — ISBN 978-1-4677-8297-5 (eb pdf)
    1. Inclined planes—Juvenile literature. 2. Levers—Juvenile literature. 3. Simple machines—Juvenile literature.
    I. Title.
TJ147.S42 2016
621.8'11—dc23   2014045361

Manufactured in the United States of America
1 – CG – 7/15/15

Table of Contents

Gus and Zach Play a Game

Gus plays with his older cousin Zach.

Zach jokes with Gus. He says Gus is too small to move him using **force**.

Gus thinks he's wrong!
How can he move Zach?

A moving truck's ramp is an inclined plane.

Gus wants to try an **inclined plane**. Inclined planes help raise and lower things.

These are all types of
simple machines.

An inclined plane is a
simple machine.

Gus tries a slide. A slide
is an inclined plane.

Zach sits at the bottom.

Gus pushes him.

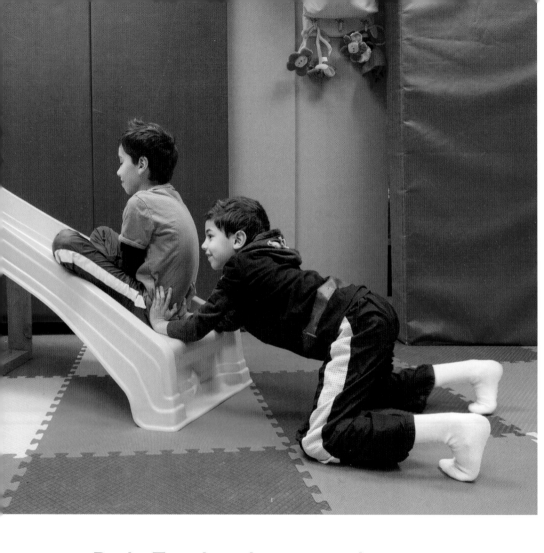

But Zach does not move.

Gus Tries a Lever

Hammers are levers that can help pull up nails.

Next, Gus tries a **lever**. Levers also can help things go up and down.

13

Levers are simple machines.

Gus tries a seesaw.
A seesaw is a lever.

The base of the seesaw is the fulcrum.

A seesaw turns on a **fulcrum**.

When one end goes down,
the other end goes up.

Zach sits on the seesaw.
He sits near the middle.

Gus sits on the end of the seesaw.

Zach moves up.

A lever helps Gus win!

How can a lever help you?

Glossary

force – pushing and pulling an object

fulcrum – the point on which a bar rests and turns

inclined plane – a flat, slanted surface

lever – a bar that lifts and lowers objects on a fixed point

simple machine – a machine with one moving part or no moving parts

Index